SUMMARY OF

WHITE FRAGILITY

WHY IT'S SO HARD FOR WHITE PEOPLE TO TALK ABOUT RACISM

By
Robin DiAngelo

**Proudly Brought to you by
John Wilder**

D1114617

Table of Contents

OVERVIEW

Those that live in North America live in a society that's grossly separated and unequal by race. Unfortunately, those who are the beneficiaries of this separation are the white people. In the United States, whites are insulated from racial stress, and we also feel that we are entitled to and deserve our advantage. Unfortunately, we haven't been able to build our racial stamina because of how rare it is for us to experience racial discomfort.

Have you ever wondered why the issue of racism has remained a problem for several decades in the United States despite perceived efforts individually and collectively to stop racism?

In what ways have our culture taught us racism and white superiority despite the belief held by most whites that we're not racists and, at the same time, making obvious racist comments or actions?

It's all about white fragility!

The process where we attempt to reinstate white equilibrium while repelling the challenge, returning to our racial comfort and maintaining our dominance in the racial hierarchy, is what I call white fragility.

"Although white fragility is often triggered by anxiety and discomfort, it is born of superiority and entitlement. White fragility is not a weakness. Rather, it is a powerful means of white racial control which helps to protect the white advantage."

The focus of this book is on the phenomenon of white fragility, various ways we develop it, how white fragility protects racial inequality, and the things we can do about it.

Are you prepared to let go of what you already know and have been taught over the years about racism and have an open mind about the topic? The things you're about to read in this book will challenge what you feel you already know. You might even discover that you've benefited from racism without being aware of it. So, if you are prepared to take a second look at racism and possibly chart a new course in your quest to foster a better relationship with people of color, then go ahead; you're in for a surprise!

Chapter 1: THE CHALLENGES OF TALKING TO WHITE PEOPLE ABOUT RACISM

We don't see ourselves in racial terms!

Key Takeaways:

- ✓ One common trigger of white fragility is being seen racially, and if white people must build their stamina, they need to deal with the first challenge, which involves naming our race.
- ✓ The opinion of whites on racism seems to be strong even when race relations are extremely complex.
- ✓ It's possible to be regarded as someone that can lead both major and minor organizations in the US without having a good understanding of views or experiences of people of color.
- ✓ The forces that condition us into racist frameworks are usually at play in our society, and interrupting such forces of racism is a lifelong work.
- ✓ Because of two Western ideologies; objectivity, and individualism, it's hard to explore these cultural frameworks.
- ✓ If truly we want to understand race relations, then we must pull out from our conditioning and deal with how and why being a member of a racial group matters.

✓ If you define a racist as someone that consciously dislikes others because of their race, then suggesting that you are a racist even when I don't know you is offensive.

As a White American that was raised in the US, I have a white worldview, a white frame of reference, and my actions in the world are based on a white experience. My experience isn't a universal human experience. Rather, it's specifically a white experience in a society that takes race seriously. A society that is grossly unequal and separate by race. But, I wasn't taught to draw attention to my race or see myself in racial terms like most individuals raised in the United States.

However, I was conscious of the fact that people's race was important, and whenever the topic of race was discussed, it wouldn't be mine but theirs. Interestingly, being able to sit with the discomfort of being seen racially and act as if our race is important (which is true) is a crucial component of cross-racial skill-building. One common trigger of white fragility is being seen racially, and if white people must build their stamina, they need to deal with the first challenge, which involves naming our race.

Our Opinions Are Uninformed

I can't recall meeting a white person that doesn't have an opinion on racism. In fact, growing up or spending significant time in the US or a culture that has a history of Western colonization without having opinions on racism is not possible. The opinion of whites on racism seems to be strong even when race relations are extremely complex. If we don't devote intentional and continuous study, then our opinions are uninformed or ignorant. The reason is that nothing in mainstream US culture provides us the information needed to possess the nuanced understanding of arguably, the most enduring and complex social dynamic of hundreds of years ago.

It's possible to be regarded as a someone that can lead both major and minor organizations in the US without having a good understanding of views or experiences of people of color; maybe had a few (if any) relationships with people of color and could not handle issues related to race. It's possible to go through graduate school or graduate from law school without even discussing the issue of racism. I might end up having just a single required "diversity" course while being in a program that is seen as progressive. In such a diversity course, there may not be any guarantee that we'll discuss anything regarding racism even though we read "ethnic" authors and learned about heroes and heroines from different groups of color.

Interestingly, white fragility usually emerges quickly when we attempt to have an open and honest discussion about race since we're often met with defensiveness, certitude, silence, argumentation, or other kinds of pushback. These kinds of responses are not natural, but social forces that deter us from acquiring the racial knowledge required to engage more productively. These forces are so powerful that they maintain the racial hierarchy. Some of these forces include meritocracy, ideologies of individualism, parochial and repetitive media representations of individuals of color, depictions of whiteness as the human ideal, jokes as well as warnings, segregation in schools and neighborhoods, white solidarity, and taboos on openly discussing the topic of race.

Since the forces that condition us into racist frameworks are usually at play in our society, interrupting such forces of racism is a lifelong work; we can never stop learning. Unfortunately, the simplistic definition of racism that we have (racism as intentional acts of racial discrimination displayed by immoral people) fosters the belief that we're never part of the problem, and there's nothing else to learn. Most of the claims we present as proofs are implausible, for instance, we often hear people say, "I was raised to treat other people the same," and others often say, *It's important that we respect one another and that begins in the home."*

The implication of such statements is that they seem to put a stop to the discussion as well as learning that could be obtained from sustained engagement. Such statements don't even convince a good number of people of color; rather, it even ends up invalidating their experiences. The next challenge that most white people have is that they don't know the process of socialization.

We Don't Understand Socialization

Every time I discuss the issue of racism with white people, it's often easy to predict their responses, and I end up feeling like we're merely reciting lines from one script. To some extent, we're reciting a common script, especially when we consider the fact that we're actors in a shared culture. A good portion of the white script is obtained from our view of ourselves as unique and objective. Understanding of the forces of socialization is essential if we must understand white fragility.

We understand our experiences and perceptions via our particular cultural lens, which is neither objective nor universal, and we require it to function in any human society. But because of two Western ideologies; objectivity, and individualism, it's hard to explore these cultural frameworks. In simple terms, objectivity informs us that we can be free from all forms of bias, while individualism implies that each of us is unique and stand apart from other people. These ideologies make it challenging for white people to explore the collective aspects of white experience.

Individualism is a belief that creates, reproduces, communicates, and reinforces this belief that we are unique persons, and each group membership like gender, race, or class is not relevant to our opportunities. It implies that individual success doesn't have intrinsic barriers, and social structures are not the cause of failure, but failure is as a result of individual character. Based on the ideology of individualism, the race is not relevant.

Although each of us occupy distinct class, gender, race as well as other positions that influence our lives, chances profoundly in ways that are not random, natural, or voluntary, an opportunity isn't uniformly distributed across gender, class or race. Although we claim that social groups aren't important and that everyone is seen as equal, it's obvious that being a man as defined by the dominant culture differs significantly from being a woman. We know that being seen as rich differs from being viewed as poor, being old is different from being seen as young, etc.

While all these groups matter, they hardly matter naturally just as we are taught to believe. We are taught to believe that they matter, and the social meaning that has been associated with such groups results in a lived experience. We learn these social meanings by a range of individuals, through a variety of mediums and in myriad ways. We continue to receive these pieces of training even after childhood and for the rest of our lives. A large chunk of this training is non-verbal, and we get them by observation and comparing ourselves with other people.

We're collectively socialized into these groups, and in mainstream culture, each of us gets similar messages regarding what each of these groups means, and reasons why being a member of each group gives an entirely different experience. Also, we now become aware that being in any of the groups is "better" than being in the opposite group. So, being rich is "better" than poor, able-bodied rather than disability. We collectively acquire an understanding of our group meaning via various shared and unavoidable aspects of the society around us like magazines, traditions, jokes, television, song lyrics, school, literature, movies, history, etc.

Our group identities are shaped by these dimensions of culture. So, the way we understand ourselves is mainly based on comparing ourselves with others. For instance, the concept of being smart doesn't mean anything without the idea of "stupid." We perceive who we are simply by understanding who we are not. Still, unfortunately, a good number of people are unskilled at reflecting on our group members because of the emphasis the society places on individuality.

If truly we want to understand race relations, then we must pull out from our conditioning and deal with how and why being a member of a racial group matter. We end up seeing the world from the perspective of a specific kind of human instead of from a universal human perspective when group membership is relevant. This ends up disrupting both ideologies. So, it's quite challenging for many whites to reflect on our racial frames since we've learned that having a racial viewpoint is to be biased.

This kind of belief ends up protecting our biases since denying their existence hinders us from examining or modifying them. This book's title will undoubtedly result in resistance for many white, and this is because I'm violating a cardinal rule of individualism – I'm generalizing. Presently, I believe that you're thinking of various ways you differ from other white people and that if only I understand the neighborhood you were raised, your experience, or how you endured this struggle, then I would believe that you're different and not a racist. This is a common reflex that I've experienced on several occasions in my work.

As a sociologist, generalizing is something I can comfortably do; social life is patterned and also predictable in measurable ways. If we are unable to explore patterns of group behavior as well as their effects on individuals, then we won't be able to understand modern forms of racism. I often encourage readers to make certain adjustments that they feel are crucial to their situation instead of rejecting the evidence completely.

Whether you were raised in Hawaii, Germany, or Canada, or there are people of color in your family, these situations can't exempt you from the forces of racism since no aspect of society can exist outside of these forces. Instead of exempting further examination because of what you perceive as unique about yourself, what would be a more fruitful approach would be asking yourself certain questions like "I'm white, and I've experienced E."

In what ways did "E" shape me because I'm white? One critical skill that can allow you to see the big picture of the society you live in is setting aside your sense of uniqueness; however, individualism will not. One of the things you can do is to set aside your narrative and deal with the collective messages that each of us gets as members of a shared culture. Examine how each of these messages has shaped your life instead of excusing yourself from the impact of these messages with some aspects of your story.

We have a Simplistic Understanding of Racism

Another major challenge that we need to deal with is how we define "racist." We've been taught in the post-civil rights era that racists are mean individuals who hate others intentionally because of their race – racists are seen as immoral. So, I'm saying something offensive when I say that all white people are racists or that my readers are racists; I'm questioning the moral character of my readers. But how can I even make such a claim when I don't even know who my readers are?

If you define a racist as someone that consciously dislikes others because of their race, then suggesting that you are a racist even when I don't know you is offensive. I also agree that you're not a racist if this is your definition of racism and that you're against racism. Well, I'm not making use of this definition of racism, and neither am I saying that you're immoral too.

Just have an open mind while I delve further into my argument, and hopefully, it would make sense soon. I strongly believe that white readers will have moments of discomfort while reading this book, and it's proof that I've somehow unsettled the racial status quo – this indeed is my goal.

What's comfortable for white people is the racial status quo, and it's not possible to progress in race relations if we remain comfortable. What we do with our discomfort is crucial to our making progress. Ask yourself these questions: what would be the implication if all this is true? How is my understanding of racial dynamics affected by this lens? In what ways can my unease assist in revealing the unexamined assumptions that I've always made before? Are there some racial dynamics that I'm unable to see because I'm white? Am I prepared to consider such a possibility, and if not, why not?

If you're reading this book and still make a case for yourself to justify why you differ from other white individuals and that this doesn't apply to you, then take a moment and breathe, then take a look at these questions and continue to work through them. If we must interrupt white fragility, then we have to develop our capacity to sustain the discomfort of being racially unmoored, the discomfort of not knowing, and the discomfort of racial humility.

Next, we need to discover how the forces of racial socialization are always at play. Our failure to acknowledge these forces results in the resistance and defensiveness of white fragility.

We need to reflect on the whole of our identities (especially our racial group identity) if we must increase the racial stamina that counters white fragility. What this means for white people is struggling with what it means to be white.

Chapter 2: RACISM AND WHITE SUPREMACY

Key Takeaways:

- ✓ The concept of race being a biological construct makes it very easy for us to accept that a good number of the divisions we notice in society are natural.
- ✓ Economic and social interests enhanced race science which established cultural norms as well as legal rulings that ended up legitimizing racism and the privileged status of individuals that are defined as white
- ✓ The concept of the white race was solidified from the late 1800s through the early twentieth century.
- ✓ People of color were first exploited before the ideology of unequal races as a way to justify exploitation that followed.
- ✓ One of the best ways to understand racism is to distinguish it from prejudice and discrimination.
- ✓ The issue of racism is deeply rooted in the fabric of our society and not just limited to one person or a single act.
- ✓ The law's construction of whiteness defines and also affirms vital aspects of identity.

A good number of us have been trained to believe that the biological and genetic make-up of each race differs significantly. So, this biology is the reason for several visual differences like hair texture, eye shape, the color of our skin, traits we believe that we see like mathematical ability, athleticism, or sexuality. The concept of race being a biological construct makes it very easy for us to accept that a good number of the divisions we notice in society are natural. But race, like gender, is socially constructed.

These differences that we identify with our eyes are superficial, and they emerged because of our adaptation to geography. Interestingly, under human skin, there is no biological race. All external features we use in defining race are not reliable indicators of genetic variation between two individuals. But, the belief that race, as well as all the differences that come with it, are biological is deep-seated. We must understand the social and economic investments that compelled science to organize society as well as its resources along racial lines and why this organization is so enduring if we must challenge the belief in race as biology.

Social Construction of Race in the United States

When the US was formed, freedom and equality (regardless of class status or religion) were radical ideas. But the economy of the United States was based on abduction and enslavement of Africans, displacement, and genocide of indigenous people as well as the annexation of Mexican lands. Also, most of these colonizers had their cultural conditioning and came with deep internalized patterns of domination and submission. The tension that existed between the noble ideology of equality and the cruel reality of enslavement, colonization, and genocide had to be reconciled.

For instance, Thomas Jefferson (who had hundreds of enslaved individuals), as well as some other individuals, embraced science. Thomas Jefferson was of the view that natural differences existed between races and requested that scientists should search for them. Science could prove that blacks were naturally inferior (he perceived indigenous people as culturally deficient, which was a shortcoming that could be resolved), then there wouldn't be a contradiction between our actual practices and professed ideals. Several economic interests existed that justified enslavement and colonization.

These economic and social interests enhanced race science, which established cultural norms as well as legal rulings that ended up legitimizing racism and the privileged status of individuals that are defined as white. While trying to know the reason for the perceived inferiority of non-Anglo groups, American Scientists failed to ask, *"Are blacks as well as others inferior?"* Instead, they asked, *"why are blacks and other races inferior?"* and Jefferson's suggestion of the existence of racial difference turned into an accepted scientific fact in less than a century.

The concept of racial inferiority was established as a means of justifying unequal treatment; it wasn't the fear of difference of the belief in racial inferiority that triggered unequal treatment. According to Ta-Neshi Coates, *"Race is the child of racism and not the father."* What he meant was that at first, people were exploited for their resources and not based on their looks. People of color were first exploited before the ideology of unequal races as a way to justify exploitation that followed.

Consumers of racist ideas have been made to accept the fact that there is something wrong with black people rather than the policies that oppressed, confined, and enslaved them. According to historian Ibram Kendi, if we genuinely believe that every human is equal, then any disparity in condition can only be a product of systemic discrimination.

The Perception of Race

The concept of race is an evolving social idea that was created to legitimize racial inequality while also protecting white advantage. The first time the term "white" appeared was in colonial law in the late 1600s. People were requested to claim their race on the census by 1790 and the perceived degrees of blood by 1825, determined those that would be regarded as Indian.

The concept of the white race was solidified from the late 1800s through the early twentieth century when more immigrants moved into the US. Whiteness maintained its importance even after slavery was abolished in the US in 1865 as there continued to be widespread legalized racist exclusion and violence against African Americans, but this time in new ways.

You had to be classified as white legally before you can have citizenship and access to the rights that come with citizenship. Individuals that had nonwhite racial classifications started petitioning the courts in a bid to be reclassified since courts can decide who was white or not. Among those who won their case to be reclassified as white were Armenians. They were assisted by a scientific witness who claimed that scientifically, they were "Caucasian."

Since the Japanese were scientifically classified as "Mongoloid," the Supreme Court in 1922 ruled that they couldn't be legally white. Well, after a year, the court also declared that Asian Indians weren't legally white despite being scientifically classified as "Caucasian." The court, in a bid to justify such contradictory rulings, declared that to be white was based on a common understanding of the white man. So, individuals that were seen as white are the ones to decide on who was white or not.

The metaphor of the US being a great melting pot where people from different parts of the world came together to melt and become a unified society via the process of assimilation is undoubtedly a cherished idea. So, as soon as new immigrants learn English and adapt to American customs and culture, they automatically become Americans. Unfortunately, during the nineteenth and twentieth centuries, those who were allowed to be assimilated into the dominant culture were the European immigrants. You now see that race is merely a social construction – people who are added to the white category change over time.

For instance, in the past, European ethnic groups like Polish, Italian, and Irish were excluded initially, but immigrants from Europe were racially united via assimilation. The assimilation process (which involves eating "American" foods, speaking English, and eliminating customs that set them apart) reified the belief of Americans as white. When it comes to the larger society, racial identification also plays a major role in identity development in the way we see ourselves. So, when someone "looks white," they are treated as white in society.

These advantages today are de facto rather than de jure; however, they are still powerful and influence our daily lives. Each of us who is regarded as a white need to identify various ways these advantages shape us instead of denying them the whole scale.

Because race is a product of social forces, you can also find it along class lines – Individuals who are poor and the working class are not seen as fully white. It's impossible to separate economic and racial forces in a society that offers fewer opportunities to individuals that are not seen as white. But as a way to exploit labor, poor and working-class whites were finally granted access into whiteness.

If whites who are poor focused more on feeling superior to individuals below them in status, they focused less on those above. If the working class as well as the poor united across race, it could result in a powerful force, however, they have been restrained from organizing against the owning class that ends up profiting from their labor courtesy of racial divisions. Don't also forget that even though working-class whites are not experiencing racism, they experience classism.

Racism

One of the best ways to understand racism is to distinguish it from prejudice and discrimination. When talking about prejudice, it has to do with pre-judgment regarding someone else based on the social groups that the individual belongs. It comprises feelings and thoughts, which include generalization, stereotypes, and attitudes that are usually based on little experience, which is projected onto others from the group. Since most of us dwell in the same cultural water and accept the same message, our prejudices are often shared.

We make sense of a particular group through our cultural framework because all humans have prejudice. Those who state that they aren't prejudiced are displaying a profound lack of self-awareness as well as the power of socialization. Even though we've been taught in schools, movies, by teachers, clergy, etc. that we shouldn't be prejudiced, the existing belief that prejudice is wrong makes us deny its unavoidable reality.

While understanding white fragility, prejudice is foundational because the suggestion that whites have racial prejudice is seen as implying that whites are bad and have to be ashamed. So, whites, in turn, will try to defend their character instead of exploring the inevitable racial prejudices they have learned over the years in a bid to change them.

When talking about discrimination, it refers to an action that's based on prejudice, and such actions include ridicule, exclusion, violence, threats, ignoring, and slander. A good number of us can acknowledge that sometimes, we are uncomfortable when we're around some groups of people or a heightened sense of self-consciousness. However, this feeling is not experienced naturally, but from living separately from a group of individuals while also accepting incomplete or wrong information regarding them. So, when the prejudices compel me to behave differently – I'm no longer very relaxed, or I try not to interact with you – then I'm discriminating.

Since the way we see the world is what drives our actions, prejudice often manifests itself in action. According to a professor of American studies and anthropology at Wesleyan University,

"When a racial group's collective prejudice is backed by the power of legal authority and institutional control, it is transformed into racism, a far-reaching system that functions independently from the intentions or self-images of individual actors."

Although each of us has prejudice and even discriminates, you should understand that the structures of oppression exceed individuals. Although women could also be prejudiced and even discriminate against men when interacting with them individually, women as a group were unable to deny men their civil rights. On the other hand, men as a group were able to deny women their civil rights because they controlled all the institutions. For women to gain suffrage, men had to grant it to them, implying that women couldn't grant themselves suffrage.

In the same vein, racism (just like sexism as well as other forms of oppression) happens anytime the racial group's prejudice gets backed by legal authority as well as an institutional control. It is the authority and control that changes individual prejudices into a system that's far-reaching and doesn't depend on the good intentions of individual actors. Instead, it turns into default of the society, which is automatically reproduced. Understand that racism is a system, and talking about the intersection of race and gender is crucial. For instance, in suffrage, full access to suffrage was granted to white women only, and women of color were denied their voting rights until the Voting Rights Acts of 1965.

The beginning of the system of racism starts with big ideas that are spread in our society even as we get conditioned from birth to accepting these ideas without questioning them. So, we find ideology being reinforced in our society via textbooks, movies, political speeches, advertising, words, and phrases as well as holiday celebrations. Since these ideas are always being reinforced, it's difficult to avoid believing and internalizing them. Some good examples of ideologies in the US include consumerism as a desirable lifestyle, individualism, democracy as a political system, superiority of capitalism as an economic system, and several others.

Also, the racial ideology that's spread in the US rationalizes racial hierarchies as the outcome of the natural order which occurred from either individual effort or talent or genetics. So, individuals that don't succeed are not naturally deserving, capable, or hardworking.

The issue of racism is deeply rooted in the fabric of our society and not just limited to one person or a single act. It doesn't move back and forth – benefiting whites now and benefiting people of color another day or even era. Racism differs from individual racial prejudice and racial discrimination in the historical accumulation and the current support of prejudice with institutional power, which even helps to systematically enforce discriminatory behaviors that have far-reaching effects.

Although people of color hold prejudices and even discriminate against white individuals, they don't have the social as well as institutional power that can help transform their prejudice and discrimination into racism. So, the effect of their prejudice on whites is contextual and temporary. White has the social and institutional positions in society to introduce their racial prejudice into policies, laws, and practices in ways that people of color can't. While people of color can wait on me if I walk into a shop, but they can't pass legislation prohibiting me and other whites from purchasing a home in a certain neighborhood.

When I say that whites can be racist, I'm implying that in the US, those who have the collective social and institutional power and privilege over people of color are whites. So, people of color lack this power and privilege over white people. Interestingly, most whites see racism as something that happened in the past, which implies that we don't get to acknowledge it in the present. But the racial disparity between people of color and whites still exists in various institutions and tends to be on the increase instead of decreasing.

Several agencies have documented the effect of these disparities on the overall quality of life like the United Nations, the US Census Bureau, and several academic groups like the Metropolis Project and the UCLA Civil Rights Project.

One of the reasons why racism is so difficult to recognize is that we have an unlimited view. We often rely on exceptions, single situations, and anecdotal evidence for our understanding instead of broader interlocking patterns. Even though their exceptions would always exist, the patterns are quite consistent and properly documented: several forces and barriers that are not avoidable, occasional, or accidental confine and shape people of color, and these forces are systematically related to each other in such a way that hinders their movement.

Although some whites may be "against" racism individually, they still derive benefits from the system, which favors whites as a group. This is what David Wellman refers to as a system of advantage that's based on race – advantages known as "white privilege." Although racism favors whites, it still does not imply that individual white people don't also encounter barriers or struggle. However, it implies that whites are not dealing with the specific barriers of racism. Racism isn't fluid; it doesn't alter its direction simply because some persons of color have been able to excel. Racism is a deeply rooted, historical system of institutional power.

Whiteness as a Position of Status

The fact that one is seen as white has implications other than mere racial classification; it further implies a social and institutional status and identity that is backed with political, economic, legal, social rights and privileges that others don't have access to. The phrase *"whiteness as property,"* as coined by Cheryl Harris, is one way to describe whiteness across legal history. Whiteness was moved from privileged identity to vested interest (external object of poverty) when it was accorded an actual legal status.

The law's construction of whiteness defines and also affirms vital aspects of identity (those who are called white), of property (the legal entitlements that are derived from the status), and of privilege (the benefits that accrue to the status). Identity is capable of granting or denying resources such as positive expectations, visibility, self-worth, etc. rather than focusing on how racism hurts people of color, which is the most common approach, it's crucial to examine whiteness by focusing on ways racism elevates whites.

White people often find it hard to see whiteness as a specific state of being, which can have an impact on one's perceptions and life. A good number of writers have been authoring books on whiteness for several decades, and these writers have encouraged white people to focus on themselves in exploring the implication of being white in a society that is seriously divided by race.

Understand that racism against people of color does not happen in a vacuum. However, the idea of racism in the US can operate outside whites; it's reinforced via celebrations like Black History Month. Such celebrations take white people out of the equation and other ways that the accomplishments of people of color are depoliticized and separated from the entire social context.

One good example of how whiteness obscures racism by making racist institutions, whites, and white privileges invisible is the story of Jackie Robinson. He is usually celebrated as the first African American to play in major league baseball. Although Robinson is an outstanding player, this story portrays him as someone that's racially special.

Let's look at the sub-context – Robinson finally was able to acquire what it takes to play with whites. This implies that there were no black athletes that were strong enough before Robinson to compete at that level. Well, another better way to tell the story is, "Jackie Robinson, the first black that whites permitted to play major league baseball." With this version, there is a clear and vital distinction because Robinson could never have played in the major leagues regardless of how skilled he is if whites didn't allow him – they practically controlled the institution.

The narratives of racial exceptionality tend to obscure the reality of the present institutional white control, which reinforces the ideologies of individualism and meritocracy. Also, they don't favor whites because they obscure the white allies that worked long and very hard behind the scenes to ensure that African American players are allowed into the field. These allies are the much-needed role models that other whites need. Don't get me wrong; I'm not against the celebration of Black History Month. I just believe that the celebration would not reinforce whiteness.

Whites have control of the major institutions of society, and they are responsible for setting the policies and practices that other people must live by. Even though several people of color have been within the circles of power (Barack Obama, Colin Powell, Marco Rubio, and others), they can only support the status quo. They can't challenge racism in a way that's threatening. There aren't shielded from racism because of their positions, and the status quo will always be intact.

Also, whites produce and even reinforce the dominant narratives of society like meritocracy and individualism and make use of these narratives to explain the positions of other racial groups. Such narratives enable us to congratulate ourselves on our achievements and success within the institutions of society while blaming other people for their lack of success. The aspect of racism favoring whites is often invisible to whites; not only are we not aware of the meaning of race and its impact on our lives, we don't also acknowledge it. So, we don't recognize or agree to white privilege as well as the norms that produce and maintain it.

This implies that to name whiteness, much less implying that it has meaning and provides an unearned advantage, will be extremely destabilizing and disconcerting, and this ends up triggering the protective responses of white fragility.

White Supremacy

We might see white supremacists as individuals we saw on television and photos bombing black churches or beating blacks at lunch counters, especially when we look back at the civil rights movement of the 1950s and 1960s. Well, since most whites don't identify with these images of white supremacists, they might take offense with the broad use of the term. White supremacy, for sociologists as well as others involved in the present racial justice movement, is a descriptive and useful term used in describing the all-encompassing centrality and assumed superiority of people that are defined and seen as white and the practices based on this assumption.

So, in this context, white supremacy refers to an overarching economic, political, and social system of domination. Don't forget that racism isn't an event but a structure. Although various hate groups that openly declare white superiority still exists, the term white supremacy also refers to them as well. This reductive definition tends to obscure the reality of the broader system, which is at play and also hinders us from dealing with this system. Indeed the US is a global power and circulates white supremacy globally via mass media, advertising, movies, military presence, missionary work, and other means.

The idea of whiteness as the ideal for humanity is promoted by this powerful ideology even beyond the West. You will find that white supremacy is mainly relevant in countries that have been formally colonized by Western nations. According to Miles, there are two factors that we need to consider that are critical to our understanding of white fragility. The first is that white supremacy is never acknowledged, and the second one is that it's impossible to study any sociopolitical system without dealing with the way that system is mediated by race. Our inability to acknowledge white supremacy not only shields it from the examination, but also keeps it in place.

Generally, race scholars make use of the term "white supremacy" in describing a sociopolitical economic system of domination that's based on racial categories, which favors individuals that are defined and seen as white. Consequently, white people are elevated as a group courtesy of a system of structural power privileges. A look at the racial breakdown of individuals that have been in control of institutions in the US between 2016 and 2017 will surprise you:

- The ten richest Americans are all whites (seven of them are among the world's ten richest)
- Current US presidential cabinet is 91 percent white
- The US Congress is made up of 90 percent white members
- The top US military advisers all white
- About 96 percent of US governors are white
- The US men's professional football teams comprise 97 percent white and several others.

All these organizations are not minor organizations – they are the most powerful in the country. It's a representation of power and control by a racial group that is positioned to disseminate and also protect its self-image and interest across the society. Media representation is one of the most viable ways white supremacy is disseminated, and it has an outstanding impact on our world view. The individuals that direct and write films are our cultural narrators, and the stories they tell are instrumental in shaping our worldviews.

Generally, white people are significantly influenced by the racial messages contained in films. For instance, in 2016, out of the hundred top-grossing films worldwide, 95 of them were directed by white Americans. Since a good number of these individuals are likely to be at the top of social hierarchy in terms of class, gender, and race, they are most unlikely to possess a broad variety of authentic egalitarian cross-racial relationships. However, they are still in the position to represent the racial "other."

So, such representations of the "other" are often parochial and problematic, but they still get reinforced repeatedly and are disseminated worldwide. We get prevented from examining how these messages shape us because of white resistance to the term white supremacy. This is something that explicit white supremacists understand.

Our provocation at the use of the term white supremacy only helps to shield the process it describes while concealing the mechanisms of racial inequality. But this word is charged, especially for older whites that link the term with extreme hate groups. It's important to note that white supremacy describes the culture that places whites as well as all that's associated with them as ideal. Two ways naming white supremacy alters the conversation.

First, it highlights this system while shifting the locus of change to whites where it belongs. Also, it helps to move us toward the direction of the lifelong work that's uniquely ours and confronts our complicity with and investment in racism. Although people of color have a part to play, those who control the institutions bear the full weight of responsibility.

The White Racial Frame

According to Joe Feagin, the "white racial frame" explains how white people circulate and reinforce racial messages to position whites as superior. So, the white racial frame rests on and is a major mechanism of white supremacy. This frame is quite extensive and deep and has lots of stored "bits" (cultural information), which includes omissions, stories, interpretations, and several others that are transferred from one individual and group to the next, from generation to generation. Also, the bits spread implicitly and explicitly through television or stories we hear from friends and family. White can reinscribe the frame even deeper by continuously making use of the white racial frame when interpreting social relations and integrating new bits.

Generally, the racial frame sees whites as superior in achievement and culture while viewing individuals of color as a less economic, political, and social consequence - seeing people of color as inferior to whites in the process of making and keeping a nation. The next level of framing, white dominance, is unremarkable and often taken for granted because social institutions like law, education, the military are controlled by whites. So, white people are entitled to more privileges as well as resources because we are "better" people. Negative stereotypes, as well as images of racial others as being inferior, are usually reinforced and accepted at the deepest level of the white frame.

This is the level where corresponding emotions like resentment, contempt, and fear are stored. When most whites reflect on their environment, the educational system where segregation exists, the way media presents information, and what they learned in school, they often discover that most of them hadn't a teacher of color until college.

On the other hand, most people of color hardly saw teachers who reflected their race(s). But why reflect on our teachers in a bid to uncover our racial socialization as well as the messages we get from schools? In school, what were you learning about the racial hierarchy as well as your position in it from geography? Race in the United States is encoded in geography. While growing up, we were taught that we all are equal; however, we don't live together across race. While growing up, I had to try and understand this separation. Why are we living separately if we were equal? It must be normal and natural to live apart (in fact, adults in my life weren't complaining about the separation).

Well, at a deeper level, since we're better people, it must be right to live apart. But how did I come to believe that we're better people? Think of the way we discuss white neighborhoods; sheltered, desirable, safe, good, and clean. So, based on this definition, other spaces that are not white are crime-ridden, dangerous and should be avoided. We may be able to discover how white children are taught how to navigate race if we add all kinds of comments we made regarding people of color privately, especially when we are less careful.

Chapter 3: RACISM AFTER THE CIVIL RIGHTS MOVEMENT

Key Takeaways:

- ✓ All systems of oppression are adaptive; they are capable of withstanding and also adjusting to different challenges while maintaining inequality.
- ✓ One example of racism's ability to adapt to cultural changes is what is termed "color-blind racism."
- ✓ What leads to averse racism is our lack of understanding of implicit bias.
- ✓ As early as preschool level, white children have already started developing a sense of shite superiority.

A film by Professor Martin Barker with the title "New racism" tried to capture various ways which racism has adapted over the years so that policies, practices and modern norms end up in similar racial outcomes just like what happened in the past and at the same time, not appearing out rightly to be racist. In the book Racism "Without Racists" by Eduardo Bonilla-Silva, while no one accepts to be a racist, the issue of racism still exists. But how possible is it for racism to exist, and no one is claiming to be a racist? One obvious reason why racism still exists is that racism is highly adaptive.

Therefore we have to identify how it changes over time, especially because of this adaptability. For instance, at the end of a nationalist march and the death of a counter-protester, the US president declared that they are "very fine people on both sides." Can you imagine a high ranking public official making such a comment? But if the president was asked if he was a racist or not, I'm so sure that his response would be a loud "No!"

The focus of this chapter is to review different ways racism has adapted over time to always yield racial disparity while exempting whites from benefiting from racism of being involved in it. First, you should understand that all systems of oppression are adaptive; they are capable of withstanding and also adjusting to different challenges while maintaining inequality. Our nation has witnessed several milestones that are worthy of celebration like the passage of the Americans with Disabilities ACT, the election of Barack Obama, the recognition of same-sex marriage, Title 9, etc.

However, you'll discover that systems of oppression are deeply rooted and can't be resolved with a simple passage of legislation. Although systems of oppression are not entirely inflexible, they are still less flexible than popular ideology would likely acknowledge.

Color-Blind Racism

One example of racism's ability to adapt to cultural changes is what is termed "color-blind racism." Based on this ideology, there can be no racism if we pretend not to notice race. This idea was based on a line from 1963 popular "I Have a Dream" speech by Martin Luther King during the March on Washington for Jobs and Freedom. It was more socially acceptable for whites to openly accept their racial prejudices as well as their belief in white superiority at the time of King's speech. Don't forget that at that time, many white people hadn't seen the level of violence that blacks experienced.

The struggle for civil rights was covered by the media, and white people watched as black men, women, and children were dragged away to lunch counters, attacked by police dogs, and suffered humiliation. With the passage of the Civil Rights Act of 1964, it became less acceptable for whites to openly admit prejudice since they don't want to be linked with the kind of dehumanizing racist acts that they saw on television in addition to the fact that discrimination was now illegal.

So, the white public took advantage of King's speech, which seemed to provide a simple and immediate solution to racial tensions: just pretend that we don't see race and racism will end. This led to the promotion of color blindness as the solution for racism with whites denying not to see race, and even if they did, it was meaningless to them. This was an indication that the civil rights movement failed to end racism, and they didn't have claims of color blindness. One popular response in the name of color blindness is stating that a person who declares that race matters is a racist – it's racist to acknowledge race.

We might look at conscious racial awareness as the tip of an iceberg, the superficial aspects of our racial socialization – people's intentions (often good), and the things we're expected to acknowledge to see (nothing). However, under the surface is the deep issue of racial socialization – associations, beliefs, internalized superiority, messages, images, emotions, perceptions, and entitlement. Because of color-blind ideology, it's often hard for us to deal with these unconscious beliefs.

Although the idea of color blindness might have initially been adopted as a well-intentioned strategy for solving the issue of racism, it led to a different result in practice. It ended up denying the reality of racism and still retain it as before. Generally, racial bias is, to a great extent, unconscious, which results in the greatest challenge – the obvious defensiveness of white people that happens anytime there is a suggestion of racial bias.

Undoubtedly, this defensiveness is a white fragility since it tends to protect our racial bias and, at the same time affirming our identities as open-minded. It's not possible to change what we have refused to see even though it's uncomfortable being confronted with things about us that we hate. There are several studies which reveal that in the workplace, people of color are discriminated against.

What do you think your coworker's response would be after being diplomatically informed or unintentionally discriminating against people of color during the hiring process? Do you think you'll be appreciated for bringing the person's attention to that issue? That's most unlikely to happen. What's likely going to happen is that your coworker would respond with anger, defensiveness, or hurt while insisting that he/she hadn't in any way discriminated, but had selected the best candidates.

Unfortunately, you would believe that this is true despite having empirical evidence that it wasn't. This defensiveness is based on the false and widespread belief that racial discrimination only manifests as intentional acts. What leads to averse racism is our lack of understanding of implicit bias.

Aversive Racism

This is a kind of racism that well-intentioned individuals who view themselves as progressive and educated are more likely to display. Aversive racism, though subtle, is an insidious form of racism because aversive racists exhibit racist acts in various ways that enable them to retain their positive self-image like "I've got many friends of color." Let's find out several ways whites enact racism and still maintain a positive self-image:

- ✓ Rationalizing that the reason why people of color don't work in our workplaces is that they don't apply.
- ✓ Rationalizing racial segregation as something that's unfortunate but essential to accessing "good schools."

- ✓ Denying the fact that there are few cross-racial relationships and going ahead to declare that our community or workplace is diverse.
- ✓ Avoiding the use of racial language and making use of racially coded terms like diverse, urban, good neighborhoods, underprivileged, sketchy, etc.
- ✓ Attributing inequality between people of color and whites to other causes apart from racism.

Averse racism is holding deep racial dislike that often manifests in our daily discourse without having to admit it simply because the hatred is in conflict with our self-image as well as the beliefs we have professed. Results of research in implicit bias has revealed that perceptions of criminal activity are usually influenced by race. Whites will sense danger merely because of the presence of black people; when it comes to race and crime, we can't trust our perceptions. Just like what Toni Morrison meant with the term "race talk," there is an explicit insertion into our daily lives of racial signs and symbols that mean nothing other than placing people of color into the lowest position of racial hierarchy.

One common component of white racial framing is casual race talk, and the reason is that it satisfies the interconnected goals of demeaning African Americans while elevating whites. In race talks, there is always a racial "us" and "them." My teacher-education students engaged in race talk, which reinforces the boundaries between "us" and them" and also position us as superior. In the process of expressing fear about finding themselves in "dangerous" neighborhoods and describing their hometowns as "sheltered," they engaged in race talk.

Such depictions are often strengthened by news stories that illustrate violent crimes committed in mainly white suburban communities as very shocking, but claiming to be raised in a sheltered environment leads to the question that has to be answered – "sheltered from what in contrast to whom?" Are we not sheltered from racist conditioning when we grow up in environments that have few or no people of color? Don't forget that in such communities, we'll need to depend on repetitive and narrow media representations, omissions, warnings, and jokes to help understand people of color.

On the other hand, they are positioning white spaces as sheltered while making the people that were raised there as racially innocent taps into classic narratives of blacks as not being innocent. You can find racist images as well as the resultant white fears at all levels of society. Several studies have shown that whites are of the view that people of color, especially blacks, are dangerous.

We feel that we're superior at a deeply internalized level and also act based on this belief daily, however, to fit into society, and maintain our self-identity as moral and good people, we need to deny this belief. But aversive racism protects just racism since we are unable to challenge our racial filters if we can't even think of having them in the first place.

Cultural Racism

The result of several research works has revealed that as early as preschool level, white children have already started developing a sense of white superiority. This should not be surprising because society frequently sends messages, which imply that being white is better than being a person of color. According to a 2014 poll that was sponsored by MTV, millennials profess more tolerance as well as a deeper commitment to fairness and equality than the previous generations did.

Also, they are committed to an ideal of color blindness that makes them uncomfortable with and even confused about race and are not in support of measures that lower racial inequality. The most outstanding aspect of the poll is that 41 percent of white millennials are of the view that minorities are getting more attention from the government. In comparison, 48 percent feel that discrimination against people of color is a problem that's as big as discrimination against whites. A good number of people believe that we're post-racial after the election of Barack Obama as president. The study by Picca and Feagin is an indication that racism is still explicitly expressed by white people, which includes the young and progressive.

On several occasions, I've been asked if I'm of the view that the younger generation is less racist, and my simple answer is NO! Racism's adaptation in some ways is more sinister than concrete rules, and such adaptations yield the same results (people of color are hindered from moving forward). Still, they have been entrenched by a dominant white society that has failed to admit to its beliefs. So, the refusal to know is another pillar of white fragility.

Chapter 4: HOW DOES RACE SHAPE THE LIVES OF WHITE PEOPLE?

White People: I don't want you to understand me better; I want you to understand yourselves. Your survival has never depended on your knowledge of the white culture. It's required your ignorance.

Key Takeaways:

- ✓ Our experiences as whites beginning from our birth will help to shape our identity as well as our worldview.
- ✓ Almost all representation of human is based on white images and norms.
- ✓ We see several concepts daily, which represents white people as the norm for humanity.

- ✓ White solidarity is the unspoken agreement that exists among all whites in a bid to protect white advantage and also not to allow a white to feel racial discomfort when they're confronted for mentioning something that's racially bad.
- ✓ We often position ourselves as innocent of race simply because we were not raised to perceive ourselves in racial terms.

It's crucial to understand the underlying foundation of white fragility if we are to understand how white people have become so difficult in conversations regarding race. We need to understand how being white influences our perspectives, our experiences, and responses. Note that all aspects of being white that we'll talk about in this section is something that's shared virtually by all-white individuals in the Western context generally and specifically, the US. Well, also note that no individual of color in this context can make such kind of claims.

Belonging

The culture I was born into was one that I belonged to racially, and I was already being shaped by the forces of racism even before I took my first breath. The hospital I was born in was because my parents are whites; the childbirth preparation class instructor was most likely a white and videos they watched in class most likely depicted whites in a class filled with whites that live in a white community. All the activities of my parents, learning, interaction, doctors, nurses, and classes were based on racial identity – all individuals involved are most likely whites.

They didn't have to worry about how they would be treated by workers in the hospital due to their race. Those who helped to maintain the facilities were likely people of color, so I entered the world in a manner that was organized hierarchically by race. In the course of my daily life, my race is unremarkable; I feel a sense of belonging when I watch the TV, learn about my country's history and its heroes and heroines, read best-selling novels, or when I see a good number of whites make the list of the "Most Beautiful." Although I may not feel inadequate considering my weight, I will belong racially.

All these experiences will help to shape my identity as well as my worldview. So, belonging has not only settled deep in my consciousness, but it also shapes my daily concerns and thoughts. The experience of belonging is just so natural that I don't need to think of it. There are rare moments in which I don't racially belong, and they're surprising, though I can either avoid them if I find them unsettling, or I simply enjoy it for its novelty.

I have always been warned to stay away from situations where I would become a racial minority, and such situations are usually described as "sketchy," dangerous, or scary. But I can be confident that I'll be viewed as racially belonging if the environment or situation is perceived as nice, valuable, or good.

Freedom From The Burden of Race

I don't need to bother about the way other people feel regarding my race, and neither do I have to carry the psychic weight of race because I've not been socialized to either see myself or be seen by other white people in racial terms. I don't have to bother about my race being held against me, and even when I might feel uncomfortable in an upper-class environment, I would easily take for granted the fact that I racially belong to these settings. I wouldn't have been stopped by George Zimmerman while walking through a gated suburban location.

Racism is in no way an issue for me, and even when I know that race has been used against people of color unfairly, I've not been trained to see it as my responsibility. Provided I've not done something that I'm aware of; racism is not an issue. I often get a feeling of racial relaxation and intellectual space because of this freedom from responsibility. This is what people of color don't enjoy in the course of their day because of being racialized within a culture of white supremacy.

Freedom of Movement

In any space that's seen as valuable, neutral, or normal, I can freely move around, and even though I may be bothered about my class status in certain settings, I don't get bothered about my race; instead, my race will work in my favor. While a person of black might feel uncomfortable staying in certain places for fear of being among racists while as a white, I don't consider any location; all locations I see as beautiful are open to me racially.

Just People

The fact that my race has been seen as the norm for humanity has also influenced my life. As whites, our race is hardly named; we're "just people." Have you wondered the number of times whites mention other people's race when they're not white? It's common to hear whites make statements like the Asian woman, my black friend, etc. Generally, writers are perceived as representing the universal human experience, and as we read books, we presume they're speaking to us.

We often go to people of color who are writers when searching for a black or Asian perspective and fall back to white writers when we're not looking for such writers, which reinforces the idea of whites as being "just human while people of color are seen as radicalized humans. Almost all representation of human is based on white images and norms – religious persons, depictions, models, and even the education of the human body, which is with blue eyes and white skin. We see several concepts daily which represents white people as the norm for humanity; whiteness as naturally superior, whiteness as the human norm and the white racial frame

White Solidarity

This is simply the unspoken agreement that exists among all whites in a bid to protect white advantage and also not to allow a white to feel racial discomfort when they're confronted for mentioning something that's racially bad. Christine Sleeter explains white solidarity as "white racial bonding," and she discovers that anytime whites interact, they often affirm *"a common stance on issues related to race, legitimating specific interpretations of groups of color and also drawing conspiratorial we-they boundaries."*

There are two aspects of white solidarity; it requires silence regarding anything that can expose the advantages of the white position and also, a tacit agreement to be united racially just to protect white supremacy. Breaking white solidarity implies breaking the rank.

You can find white solidarity at parties, dinner tables, and also in the workplace. Most of us even find ourselves saying things that are racially offensive at dinner time, and even when everyone cringes, no one eventually challenges us simply because no one wants to ruin the dinner. This also applies to parties or the workplace, and they are examples of white solidarity. The real aftermath of violating white solidarity plays a key role in helping to maintain white supremacy. Sometimes, we risk criticism as well as other penalties from other whites and may be accused of being incorrect politically.

Also, we may be seen as combative or angry, and such penalties for breaking white solidarity has caused me to be silent too often in a bid to be liked or to avoid conflict. But what happens when I keep quiet about racism? I get rewarded, of course, with social capital like being seen as cooperative, a team player, or being seen as fun. So, in white supremacist society, I can be punished in several ways for interrupting racism and rewarded for not doing so in various ways. But every single uninterrupted racial joke furthers the circulation of racism via culture, and my complicity determines if the joke would circulate. You should bear in mind that people of color experience white solidarity as a kind of racism – failing to hold each other accountable and challenge racism anytime we see it.

The Good Old Days

I can openly and unabashedly recall the "good old days" as a white person and collections of the past, and a desire for a return to former ways is simply a function of white privilege. This usually manifests in the ability to be oblivious to our racial history. Believing that the past was socially better than the present is undoubtedly a sign of white supremacy. Any period in the past for people of color is full of tales they never wish to remember again; black women being raped for the pleasure of whites, 246 years of brutal enslavement, attempted genocide of Indigenous people, and several others.

A look at past events from the perspective of people of color would reveal how a romanticized past is purely a white construct. Unfortunately, this is a strong construct since it points to a deeply internalized sense of superiority as well as entitlement and a sense that the advancement of people of color encroaches to this entitlement. Also, the romanticized "traditional" family values that we had in the past are racially problematic. To escape the influx of people of color, white families moved away from cities to the suburbs, which is often regarded by sociologists as white flight.

Then, they wrote covenants to ensure that schools and neighborhoods are segregated, and cross-racial dating was forbidden. It has not always been African Americans that resist integration efforts but white people. The idealization of the past, at the minimum, is another instance of white experiences and perceptions portrayed as universal. How do you think this nostalgia will sound to people of color that know of the history of this country?

The ability to wipe out this racial history and even accept that the past was much better than the present for all of us has given me a false consciousness personally and also as a national citizen.

White Racial Innocence

We often position ourselves as innocent of race simply because we were not raised to perceive ourselves in racial terms or see white space as racialized space. I've heard whites on several occasions claim that they were sheltered from race, and that's why they grew up in segregation.

At the same time, whites turn to people of color who were possibly raised in racially segregated spaces because of decades of policies that prevented them from moving into white neighborhoods to learn about racism. People of color are not often perceived as racially innocent, and that's why they are expected to talk about issues of race (only on white terms). The reason why people of color take extreme risks of invalidation and retaliation while sharing their experiences is because of the idea that racism is not a white problem.

Since they – not we – have race, people of color are the holders of racial knowledge. Another aspect of white racial innocence is white flight because it's usually justified by beliefs that people of color (especially African Americans) are more prone to commit crimes, so crime will increase if "too many" blacks move into a neighborhood; it will increase the rate of crime, lower the value of homes and lead to the deterioration of the neighborhood. For most white people, the percentage of young men of color living in a neighborhood is directly correlated with perceptions of neighborhood crime levels.

But the history of the extensive and brutal violence of white against blacks, as well as their ideological rationalizations, are usually trivialized via white claims of racial innocence. It's been properly documented that blacks, as well as Latinos, are stopped more often by police than whites for similar activities, and they even get harsher sentences than whites for a similar crime. It has also been revealed by research that a primary reason for this racial disparity can be attributed to the beliefs that judges and others hold regarding the cause of criminal behavior.

It's a major effort for those of us that focus on raising racial consciousness of whites because it's often hard to get whites to acknowledge the advantage our race gives us. Another aspect of white racial innocence that usually reinforces various problematic racial assumptions is the expectation that people of color need to teach white people about racism. It means that racism is something that happens to people of color and doesn't concern whites, so we can't be expected to have any knowledge of it. This setup ends up denying the fact that racism is a relationship where both parties are involved. Leaving it to people of color to deal with racial issues, ends up relieving whites of the tensions as well as the social dangers of openly speaking to them.

Segregated Lives

Undoubtedly, life in the US is grossly shaped by racial segregation, and whites are the most likely to embrace segregation and be in the social and economic position to do so too. Being raised on segregation only reinforces the message that our experiences and perspectives are the only ones that count. When it comes to poor urban whites, segregation is usually lessened since white poverty brings whites close to people of color. It's most likely that the most profound message of racial segregation is that the absence of people of color from the lives of whites is no significant loss.

Some white people could live their entire lives without a loved one of color or friend and not regard it as a diminution of their life. Whites are taught that nothing of value is lost through segregation. So, our socialization engenders a common set of racial patterns that form the foundation of white fragility. Some of these patterns include:

- We see ourselves as people that are exempt from the forces of racial socialization.
- The lack of racial humility as well as the unwillingness to listen.
- A lack of understanding about the meaning of racism.
- Failing to acknowledge that we bring the history of our group with us and that history matters.
- Confusing disagreement with not understanding.
- Overlooking the things that we don't grasp.
- Having the need to keep white solidarity to look good.

5: THE GOOD/BAD BINARY

He's not a racist. He is a really nice guy.

Key Takeaways:

- ✓ Saying that someone is a racist often appears like a character assassination, which causes them to defend themselves instead of reflecting on their behavior.
- ✓ Individual racists are part of a larger system of interlocking dynamics.
- ✓ The idea that racism is just individual intentional acts that are done by people who aren't kind is a root cause of white defensiveness. If we must overcome white defensiveness, then we need to discard this common belief.

The focus of this chapter is on what in recent history is probably the most effective adaptation of racism – the good/bad binary. Before the civil rights movement, it was generally acceptable for whites to openly express their belief in their racial superiority. Still, the images of black brutality and violence became the archetypes of racists. It's not possible to be a good person while engaging in something associated with such violence – only bad individuals were racists. It was the black persecution that happened in the north during the civil rights movement that resulted in the positioning of racists as Southern by Northern whites.

Before this adaptation, racism needed to be reduced to isolated, simple, and extreme acts of prejudice which must be malicious and intentional – a conscious dislike of a person because of race. So, those white individuals in the South that post "Whites Only" signs over fountains were the racists. The well-intended people, open-minded individuals that were raised in the "enlightened North," can't be racists. Although making racism appear as something bad seemed like a good development, it's crucial to find out how it functions in practice.

Saying that someone is a racist often appears like a character assassination, which causes them to defend themselves instead of reflecting on their behavior. The good/bad binary is what made it extremely difficult for an average white to even understand racism and impossible to interrupt it. This good/bad frame is undoubtedly a false dichotomy. Every one of us holds prejudices, especially when it has to do with race in our society that's grossly divided by race. If we must change our perspectives about racism, then we have to carry out a sincere evaluation of how racism manifests in our lives as well as in society.

Individual racists are part of a larger system of interlocking dynamics. The personal, cultural, and structural analysis that's required to challenge this larger system is often masked by the focus on individual incidences. The idea that racism is just individual intentional acts that are done by people who aren't kind is a root cause of white defensiveness. If we must overcome white defensiveness, then we need to discard this common belief. Understanding the structural nature of racism is obscured by the good/bad binary, and this makes it difficult to understand.

If you're a white person and at some point, you've been challenged to assess your racism, it's common to feel defensive. All your energy will be directed toward denying the possibility that you're a racist instead of trying to identify what you said or did wrongly. You will respond with white fragility, which only shields the problematic attitude that you're so defensive about. This can be seen in various cases where people make shockingly racist statements and still insist that they're not racists.

Over the years, I've heard several claims repeatedly made by whites, which are rooted in the good/bad binary. I classified these claims into two categories: The first one has to do with claims of color blindness – I'm free from racism because I don't see color (race is meaningless to me). The second set are those that claim to value diversity – I've got people of color as friends, and I've been near them, so I'm not a racist. These two categories rest on the good/bad binary, and as I attempt to unravel how these claims work, one question remains crucial to me; *"Are these claims true or false?"*

Most of these racial claims are often based on an underlying framework of meaning. We'll learn how we manage to make such claims in the context of extreme segregation and racial inequity by identifying this framework. A good number of us that were alive before and during the 1960s would not doubt having images of the civil rights conflicts, which now seem like the epitome of racism. Also, we now have the images of white nationalists marching in Charlottesville, Virginia, to hold up as well.

Even though speaking against these explicitly racist actions is essential, care must be taken so that we don't end up using them to keep ourselves on the "good" side of the false binary. The issue of racism has been deeply woven into the fabric of society we live in that I don't think I can ever escape from the continuum. However, I believe that I can always make efforts to move further along it. Conceptualizing myself on an active continuum switches the question from whether I am a racist or not to; *"Am I actively working toward interrupting racism in this context and how do I know if I'm doing it?"*

Chapter 6: ANTI-BLACKNESS

But all our phrasing—race relations, racial chasm, racial justice, racial profiling, white privilege, even white supremacy—serves to obscure that racism is a visceral experience, that it dislodges brains, blocks airways, rips muscle, extracts organs, cracks bones, breaks teeth. . . You must always remember that the sociology, the history, the economics, the graphs, the charts, the regressions all land, with great violence, upon the body.

—Ta-Nehisi Coates, Between the World and Me

Key Takeaways:

✓ Discussing race as well as racism in general terms like white people is constructive for whites since it helps to interrupt individualism.

✓ The culture we live in is one that circulates relentless messages depicting white superiority, which exists at the same time with constant messages of black inferiority.

✓ Anti-blackness is foundational to our identities as whites.

✓ Research attests to the fact that there is a white disdain for blacks, from school-to-prison pipeline to mass incarceration, to white flight.

- ✓ The early American economy was developed based on slave labor, and even the Capitol, as well as the White House, were also built by slaves.
- ✓ Whites are drawn to blacks who cast their eyes downward in our presence, those we feel we can "save" from the horrors experienced as blacks with our kindness and abundance.

The issue of racism is a complex and nuanced one that manifests differently for every group of color. If whites must challenge the ideologies of racism like color blindness and individualism, then we need to suspend our perception of ourselves as outside race and unique race. We interrupt a major privilege of dominance when we explore our collective racial identity. We must discuss white people as a group to help disrupt our unracialized identities. We also don't need to take for granted the privilege of people of color to see themselves or be seen as unique individuals outside the context of race.

Discussing race as well as racism in general terms like white people is constructive for whites since it helps to interrupt individualism. However, racial generalization ends up reinforcing something else, which is problematic for people of color, and that's the continual focus on their group identity. Besides, it merges other racial groups into one generic category, and this ends up denying the specific ways every group experiences racism.

This chapter will focus on addressing the uniquely anti-black sentiment integral to white identity. This doesn't in any way lower the racist experience of other groups of people of color, though, in the white mind, I'm convinced that blacks are the ultimate racial *"other."* So, it's a foundational aspect of the racial socialization underlying white fragility, and we just have to grapple with this relationship.

Please note that I'm discussing white people at the societal level. I don't suppress my feelings of hatred and contempt when sitting with blacks; I have black friends that I love deeply; when I see them, I see their humanity. However, I would also note that on the macro level, there is this deep anti-black feeling that I've learned since childhood. Such feelings surface immediately even before I have time to think anytime I look at blacks in general. I experience the sentiments when I meet black strangers on the street; I notice stereotypical depictions of blacks in media and hear jokes by whites.

So, I need to properly examine these deeper feelings, which can manifest unconsciously and hurt people that I love. As earlier mentioned, the culture we live in is one that circulates relentless messages depicting white superiority, which exists at the same time with constant messages of black inferiority. However, anti-blackness is much deeper than the negative stereotypes that we all have absorbed.

We should understand that anti-blackness is foundational to our identities as whites. Interestingly, whiteness for a long time has constantly been predicated on blackness. The concept of white race or race, in general, emerged to justify the enslavement of Africans, and the moment we created an inferior black race, we also created a superior white race as well. One can't exist without the other

This implies that whites need blacks – the creation of white identity depends on blackness. Most scholars are of the view that white people split off from themselves and usually project onto blacks several aspects we're not ready to own in ourselves. For instance, white masters of African slaves often portrayed them as childlike and lazy while they worked from sunup to sundown.

Presently, we depict people of color (especially blacks) as dangerous, and this depiction ends up perverting the actual direction of violence between blacks and whites since the founding of the United States. What I'm referring to is the collective white consciousness, and it's hard for an individual white to be explicitly conscious of such feelings, but they often emerge with the slightest challenge.

Take a look at the enduring white resentment regarding the perceived injustices of affirmative action programs. Empirical evidence exists to confirm that there has been discrimination against people of color (mostly blacks) in hiring since enslavement ended. Many people are misinformed about affirmative action, which is evidenced in the idea of special rights. For instance, it's commonly believed that people of color must be hired before a white person if they apply for a position.

This implies that blacks are given preferential treatment in the hiring process and that a particular number of people of color need to be hired just to fill a quota. Well, these beliefs are patently not true. The truth is that affirmative action is just a tool that ensures that qualified minority applicants are offered similar employment opportunities as whites. So, it's a flexible program (without requirements or quotas) as commonly believed. Unfortunately, this program has been systematically eroded. In some states, affirmative action programs have been eliminated, and at the organizational leadership level, blacks have remained a grossly underrepresented group.

Research attests to the fact that there is a white disdain for blacks, from school-to-prison pipeline to mass incarceration, to white flight. There have been cases of white flight that's triggered when formerly white neighborhoods have 7 percent blacks in them. The American Sociological Foundation in a 2015 study discovered that the highest level of segregation in the United States is between blacks and whites, while the lowest is between Asians and whites.

One of the most common ways we see anti-black sentiment is in how quickly pictures of brutality toward black children are often justified by the white assumption that such brutality must have been deserved. Such beliefs would undoubtedly be unimaginable if the images shown were that of white kindergartens handcuffed, or the shooting of a white child while playing with a toy gun. We also see anti-blackness in the level of the harshness of the criticism of blacks by every measure.

Unfortunately, we tend to forget that the early American economy was developed based on slave labor, and even the Capitol, as well as the White House, were also built by slaves. A sincere evaluation of America's relationship to the people of color (mostly the black family) reveals that the country is not its nurturer; rather, its destroyer, which didn't end with slavery. Anti-blackness is deeply grounded in misinformation, projections, lies, fables, and perversions. It's also rooted in a lack of historical knowledge as well as an inability or unwillingness to link the effects of history to what is happening presently.

Another form of racialized trauma, which is quite different from the others but equally real, lives in the bodies of most whites in the United States. It's our projections that enable us to bury this trauma by dehumanizing and going ahead to blame the victims. If African Americans aren't human just as whites, our mistreatment of them doesn't count. There is a curious satisfaction in the punishment of blacks – the satisfaction of whites as they observe the mass incarceration as well as the execution of blacks presently.

I would bluntly state here that the white collective fundamentally dislikes blackness because of what it reminds us of – that as whites, we're capable and equally guilty of carrying out unimaginable harm, and whatever gains we have was from the subjugation of others. We also have this strong hatred for "uppity" African Americans that dare to stand out and look us in the eyes as equals. The kind of messages that constantly circulate across generations often reinforces the belief by whites that blacks are inherently underserving (this is outrageous and underserving considering the state-sanctioned robbery of black labor).

According to Carol Anderson, *"the trigger for white rage, inevitably, is black advancement. It is not the mere presence of black people that is the problem; rather, it is blackness with ambition, with drive, with purpose, with aspirations, and with demands for full and equal citizenship. It is the blackness that refuses to accept subjugation, to give up."* Anti-blackness is a quite complex and equally confusing mix of resentment and benevolence even as you discover that whites use blacks to feel warmhearted and noble.

Whites are drawn to blacks who cast their eyes downward in our presence, those we feel we can "save" from the horrors experienced as blacks with our kindness and abundance. White racial socialization establishes several conflicting feelings toward blacks – hatred, resentment, benevolence, superiority, and guilt all exist below the surface and at the slightest breach, and they erupt even though they can never be openly acknowledged. The urge in us to deny the bewildering displays of anti-blackness that exists close to the surface causes us to be irrational, and it's that irrationality that forms the core of white fragility and the pain it causes African Americans.

Chapter 7: RACIAL TRIGGERS FOR WHITE PEOPLE

Key Takeaways:

- ✓ Whites hardly find themselves without the protective pillows of resources and benefit of the doubt.
- ✓ Intense emotional reactions are common whenever ideologies like meritocracy, individualism, and color blindness are challenged.
- ✓ A good number of whites possess very limited information regarding the meaning of racism and the way it works.

All the factors that we earlier discussed in the previous chapter shield whites from race-based stress. While white people's racial insulation is in some ways mediated by social class (generally, the less racially insulated are the poor and working-class urban whites), the larger social environment often shields white people as a group via cultural representations, school textbooks, institutions, advertising, movies, and several others. Observe that whites hardly find themselves without the protective pillows of resources and benefit of the doubt.

While enjoying the insulated environment of racial privilege, whites expect racial comfort and are often less tolerant of racial stress. Intense emotional reactions are common whenever ideologies like meritocracy, individualism, and color blindness are challenged. Some of the reasons why white people are often very defensive regarding the suggestion that we derive benefits from and are also complicit in a racist system include:

- Fear and resentment toward people of color
- The social taboos against openly discussing race
- The guilty knowledge we have that there's more happening than we can or will admit to
- A deep cultural legacy of anti-black sentiment
- The white delusion that we're objective people
- Having an internalized superiority as well as a sense of a right to rule.

Unfortunately, a good number of whites possess very limited information regarding the meaning of racism and the way it works. An isolated course that was taken in college might be the only time in their life they might have an encounter as well as a direct, sustained challenge to their racial identity. Even with such training, most don't discuss racism directly, let alone talk about white privilege.

Such training and workplace programs, which often come more often, make use of racially coded languages like "disadvantaged," "inner-city," and "urban." It's rare to see such training use words like "privileged," "white," or "over-advantaged." Such racist images and perspectives are reproduced by racially coded language. At the same time, racially coded language reproduces the comfortable illusion that race, as well as its challenges, are what "they" are experiencing and not us.

We can conceptualize white fragility as a response or "condition," which is produced or reproduced by continual social and material advantages of being white. Anytime there is a disequilibrium – a situation where there is an interruption to what's familiar and taken for granted – equilibrium will be restored by white fragility, and also the capital "lost" through the challenge will be restored as well. This capital includes control, white solidarity, and self-image.

There is often a wave of anger toward the trigger, outrightly shutting down and tuning out indulgence in emotional incapacitation like "hurt feelings" or guilt, exiting, or even a combination of these responses results. It's important to note that these strategies are seldom conscious; they are mainly reflective, but this doesn't justify them or make them acceptable.

Chapter 8: THE RESULT: WHITE FRAGILITY

Key Takeaways:

✓ As early as preschool, a sense of white superiority and knowledge of racial power codes have already begun to develop in white children.

✓ Since these white children are raised to experience their racially based advantages as normal and fair, they hardly get any kind of instruction about the predicament they're facing much less any form of guidance regarding how they can resolve it.

✓ Whites often makes use of terms that connote physical abuse in tapping into the classic story that African Americans are dangerous and violent.

✓ Our refusal to directly acknowledge this race talk leads to a split of consciousness, which further results in irrationality and incoherence.

✓ White fragility keeps people of color "in their place," and this makes it a powerful form of white racial control.

According to a poll that was released from NPR, the Robert Wood Johnson Foundation and the Harvard T. H. Chan School of Public health, a good number of whites are of the view that presently, there is discrimination against them in the United States. 55 percent of whites that were surveyed stated that overall, they are convinced that there is discrimination against whites in the United States today. It's also important to take note of the fact that even though more than half of white people in the poll believe that there's an existence of discrimination, the percentage that says they have indeed experienced it is much smaller.

Also, a large body of research regarding children and race reveals that they begin to construct their ideas about race at a very early age. It's remarkable to note that as early as preschool, a sense of white superiority and knowledge of racial power codes have already begun to develop in white children. According to professor of communications, Judith Martin, just like other Western nations, the children of whites born in the US inherit the moral predicament of having to live in a white supremacist society.

Since these white children are raised to experience their racially based advantages as normal and fair, they hardly get any kind of instruction about the predicament they're facing much less any form of guidance regarding how they can resolve it. Consequently, they experience or discover about racial tensions without identifying Euro-Americans' historical responsibility for it. They know virtually nothing regarding the contemporary roles they play in perpetuating it too.

Regardless of its ubiquity, you will find that white superiority is unnamed, and most whites deny it. When we become adults that completely oppose racism just like many others out there, we usually organize our identity around a denial of our privileges that we enjoy courtesy of racism and even reinforce racist disadvantage for others. Probably the most challenging aspect of this contradiction is the fact that whites' moral objection to the issue of racism ends up increasing their resistance to acknowledging their complicity with it.

In the context of a white supremacist, white identity usually depends on a foundation of (superficial) race tolerance and acceptance. Most times, a good number of whites that position themselves as liberal usually choose to shield the things they see as their moral reputation, so we end up focusing on recognizing or modifying our participation in systems of domination and inequity.

One of the ways whites tend to protect their positions anytime we're challenged on race is involving the discourse of self-defense. In the course of this discourse, white often portrays themselves as victimized, blamed, slammed, and attacked. Also, the self-defense strategy reinscribes racist imagery. Since they usually position themselves as the victims of anti-racial efforts, they can't, at the same time, become beneficiaries of whiteness.

They claim that they are the ones that have been unfairly treated – through a challenge to their position or expecting that they listen to the perspectives as well as experiences of people of color – so, they are justified in demanding that more social resources like attention and time be pushed in their direction to help them in coping with the perceived mistreatment. The language of violence that a good number of white people use when describing antiracist endeavors has some significance, and it's a good example of how white fragility distorts reality.

Whites often make use of terms that connote physical abuse in tapping into the classic story that African Americans are dangerous and violent. Through this process, whites distort the actual direction of danger between whites and other people. The use of the language of violence helps to reveal how fragile and ill-equipped most whites are in confronting racial tensions as well as their subsequent projection of this tension onto blacks and people of color in general. But, whites still engage in racial discourse, but do so under controlled conditions.

After noticing the racial positions of racial others, we then freely talk about it among ourselves but often in coded ways. Our refusal to directly acknowledge this race talk leads to a split of consciousness, which further results in irrationality and incoherence. Also, this denial ensures that the racial misinformation which influences our culture and even frames our perspectives will not be examined. White equilibrium can be described as a cocoon of racial comfort, superiority, centrality, racial apathy, obliviousness, and entitlement; all these are rooted in an identity of being good individuals that are free of racism.

A challenge to this cocoon will offset our racial balance. Whites haven't had the chance to build the capacity to sustain the discomfort associated with being off our racial balance because being racially off-balance is not common. So, as whites, we find such challenges difficult to bear and hope that they would stop.

White Fragility As a Form of Bullying

You should note that although our capacity as white people to sustain challenges to our racial positions is limited (in this way, fragile), the outcome of our responses is in no way fragile; instead, they are very powerful since they leverage historical and institutional power and control.

We possess this control and power in any way possible that's most useful in that particular moment to help protect our positions. So, just to make sure that attention is diverted away from a discussion of our racism, we can even go to the extent of crying (a technique often used by white middle-class women) just to make sure that all the resources rush back to us. If we must argue, minimize, play devil's advocate, tune out, withdraw, or pout in a bid to stop the challenge, then we will do that. So, white fragility acts like a kind of bullying, making it so miserable for others to confront us (regardless of how diplomatically they try to do so) that they just end up backing off, never talking about the issue again or completely giving up.

You should bear in mind that white fragility keeps people of color "in their place," and this makes it a powerful form of white racial control. We can think of the triggers of white fragility, which we've discussed before in the previous chapter as challenges to white power and control and of white fragility as the means to end the challenge while keeping that control and power. I need to point out here that the phrase "white fragility" is meant to describe a very specific white phenomenon; it exceeds mere defensiveness or whining.

It can also be conceptualized as the sociology of dominance – the result of whites' socialization into white supremacy, which is meant to maintain, protect, and reproduce white supremacy. It's a term that does not apply to other groups that may register complaints. It would be revolutionary for people of color to give white people feedback, then allow whites to receive it, reflect on it, and work toward making changes to the behavior. This, in the words of a man of color, in one of my workshops, would be revolutionary.

While asking my fellow whites to ponder on that response, the response revealed how hard and fragile we are as well. Also, it discloses how easy it can be to take responsibility for our racism. But, if we continue to operate from a dominant worldview that those who engage in racism are intentionally mean people, then we're not likely going to get there soon.

Chapter 9: WHITE FRAGILITY IN ACTION

Key Takeaways:

- ✓ When whites' assumptions and behaviors are challenged, we feel attacked, challenged, angry, etc.
- ✓ In response to the feelings, we engage in certain behaviors like avoiding, physically walking out, crying, or arguing.
- ✓ White fragility makes whites the victim; it silences discussion and maintains white solidarity.

I've found myself as someone that's in a position to offer feedback to whites regarding the way their unintentional racism is being manifested because of my profession as a consultant and facilitator. Also, this position has helped me to see several enactments of white fragility, and one of the most popular ones is outrage: *"why on earth would you dare suggest that I could have said or done something racist?"* I find this both unpleasant and also amusing. All through this book, I've tried to reveal the inevitable racist assumptions that whites hold and patterns they display, which are conditioned by living in a white supremacist culture.

Anytime these patterns are mentioned or questioned, our responses are usually predictable. Most of those responses start with various unexamined assumptions which, when properly examined, can cause different emotions that lead to some expected behaviors. We then proceed to justify these behaviors with several claims.

When whites' assumptions and behaviors are challenged, what are some of the popular emotional reactions that we have? We feel:

- Silenced
- Angry
- Insulted
- Attacked
- Shamed
- Scared
- Singled out
- Judged
- Outrage
- Guilty

Anytime we experience such feelings listed above, some of our common responses are to behave in any of the following ways:

- Physically walking out
- Denying
- Crying
- Avoiding
- Arguing
- Physically leaving
- Focusing on intentions

- Withdrawing emotionally
- Seeking absolution

Since most of these responses and reactions are strong emotions, they have to be justified. So, what are the claims we often make to justify such behaviors and feelings? Well, the claimant often comes up with some claims to suggest that they have been accused of falsely, while others indicate that the claimant is more knowledgeable than the discussion (I know all this already). Others are:

- This is just your opinion
- You misunderstood me
- You're judging me
- I merely said one small innocent thing
- I disagree
- You're not doing this the right way
- I don't feel safe
- I can't say anything
- You don't know me
- You're generalizing

It's common to see people who claim to have lived through things that I haven't lived through, which serves to justify the fact that there isn't anything that I can ever tell them regarding race.

Assumptions

Okay, let's dig deep and examine the framework of various assumptions that most of the claims made rest on:

- I'm free of racism.
- Racism can only be intentional, so the absence of intentional racism in my life offsets the impact of my behavior.
- I will be the judge of whether racism has occurred.
- My sufferings and pains relieve me of racism.
- My learning is finished; I know all I need to know.
- I can't be a racist because I'm a good person.
- As a white person, I fully understand the best ways to challenge racism.
- There is no problem; society is cool the way it is.
- It's unkind to point out racism.
- Racists are bad people; so, are you implying that I'm bad?

These are some of the underlying assumptions that engender these behaviors, feelings, and claims, but how do they function?

Functions of White Fragility

- They maintain white solidarity.
- Make whites the victim.
- Protect white privilege.
- Close off self-reflection.

- Silence discussion.
- Take the issue of race off the table.
- Trivialize the reality of racism.
- Protect a limited worldview.
- Rally more resources to whites.
- Hijack, the conversation.

These behaviors, as well as the undergirding assumptions, do not in any way present the claimant as someone that's racially open; instead, it's the opposite. They end up blocking all entry points for engagement and reflection. This is taken further as they also hinder their ability to amend a racial breach. They enhance racial divisions while filled with resentment and hostility. So, in conclusion, racism is engendered by the prevailing white racial assumptions as well as their behaviors.

Chapter 10: WHITE FRAGILITY & THE RULES OF ENGAGEMENT

Key Takeaways:

- ✓ Racism is the norm instead of an aberration, and feedback is crucial to our ability to identify and amend our inevitable and frequent unaware collusion.
- ✓ Also, white fragility is evidenced in the urge for many white progressives to "build trust" before exploring racism in support groups and workshops.
- ✓ The only way one can offer feedback without really triggering white fragility is by not offering any feedback at all

Since racism has been highly conceptualized as individual acts of cruelty, it, therefore, implies that it's only those terrible individuals who consciously dislike people of color that can enact racism. Although this conceptualization is misinformed, it's not benign. It acts effectively to make it almost impossible to get involved in necessary dialogue and self-reflection that can lead to a change. Most times, the outrage shown by whites at the suggestion of racism is usually preceded by righteous indignation regarding the way the feedback was provided.

After working with my fellow whites for several years, I've noticed (just like many people of color) that there are several unspoken rules for the way people are expected to give whites feedback on our inevitable, as well as most frequent unconscious racist assumptions and patterns. I have also discovered that the only way one can offer feedback without really triggering white fragility is by not offering any feedback at all. This makes the first rule cardinal:

Never offer me feedback on my racism under any circumstances.

Well, you may have to follow these rules if you break the cardinal rule:

- Appropriate tone is essential – you need to give your feedback calmly. The feedback would be invalid and may even be dismissed if you display any emotion.
- Trust needs to be between us. So, you need to trust that I'm in no way a racist before providing feedback on my racism.
- You need to offer the feedback immediately. If you wait for too long, it might be discounted because it wasn't offered sooner.
- The relationship between us must be free from issues – don't give me feedback on racism until all unrelated issues in existence are settled.
- Feedback needs to be given privately, regardless of whether the incidence took place right in front of others. It's a serious social transgression to give feedback in front of other people who were involved in the situation. If you're unable to protect me from

embarrassment, then the feedback will be invalid, and you will become a transgressor.

- As a white, I need to feel entirely safe in the course of a discourse on race. I'll feel unsafe when you suggest that I've got racist assumptions, and you'll need to rebuild my trust by not providing me feedback. What I mean here by "safe" is "comfortable."

- You end up invalidating the form of expression that I often experience, such as heterosexism, classism, ageism, transphobia, etc. by highlighting my racial privilege. So, we'll now have to focus on how you oppressed me.

- By suggesting that my behavior possessed a racist impact is misunderstanding me. You'll allow me to explain myself until you can now acknowledge that you're the one that misunderstood me.

- You need to acknowledge my intentions (which are always nice) and also accept that my good intentions offset the impact of my behavior.

Interestingly, the contradictions in most of these rules are not relevant; instead, they serve to obscure racism, regain equilibrium, and shield white dominance, which they do quite effectively. But where did these rules come from, and who do they serve?

Racism is the norm instead of an aberration, and feedback is crucial to our ability to identify and amend our inevitable and frequent unaware collusion. So, based on this understanding, I endeavor to follow certain guidelines:

- I have realized that how, where, and when you give me feedback is not relevant; instead, what I want is the feedback. Since I know that it's difficult to give, I will accept it in any way I can get it. Based on my position of cultural, social, and institutional white power as well as privilege, I'm quite safe, and I can handle it, but if I can't, I must build my racial stamina.
- Thank you.

The basis for this guideline is because there is no face to save, and the game is up. I acknowledge that I've got blind spots as well as unconscious investments in racism. I didn't create this system, but it favors me, and I use it often to my advantage, and I have to interrupt it.

Also, white fragility is evidenced in the urge for many white progressives to "build trust" before exploring racism in support groups and workshops. It's crucial to note that stopping our racist patterns has to be more crucial than trying to convince other whites that we don't even have such patterns. We have them, and people of color are already aware that whites have them – we're not convincing enough at our attempts to prove otherwise.

Chapter 11: WHITE WOMEN'S TEARS

But you are my sister, and I share your pain!

Key Takeaways:

- ✓ White women's tears wield a strong impact that tends to reinscribe instead of ameliorating racism.
- ✓ Being ignorant or insensitive to this history is a good example of white centrality, lack of racial humility, and individualism.
- ✓ I've seen our tears manipulate men of all races through the result of this manipulation are not always the same.
- ✓ Our racial socialization causes us to repeat racist behavior regardless of our self-image or intentions.

By "white tears," I mean various ways – both metaphorically and literally – that white fragility shows itself via white people's laments over how hard the issue of racism is on us. Based on the experience of my work, I usually encounter such tears in different forms. A good number of writers have provided amazing critiques as well. I'm convinced that expressing our heartfelt emotions (those related to racial injustices in particular) is a valuable progressive value.

Repressing our feelings may be counterintuitive to being present, supportive, and compassionate. White women's tears wield a strong impact that tends to reinscribe instead of ameliorating racism. Emotions for most of us occur naturally, but they are also political in two significant ways. Our emotions are usually framed by our beliefs and biases, as well as our cultural frameworks.

For instance, if I believe that racists are strictly bad people, I'll definitely be hurt, shamed, and offended anytime an unaware racist assumption of mine is identified by someone else. However, if I'm of the view that having racist assumptions is inevitable (but can be changed), I'll be grateful when I'm notified of an unaware racist assumption of mine. This way, emotions are natural, and they are the consequence of the frameworks we use when making sense of social relations.

There are several reasons why white women's tears in cross-racial interactions are problematic, and the reasons are connected to how they impact other people. History is filled with cases of black men that were tortured and even killed simply as a result of a white woman's distress, and white women bring these histories with us. The tears of white women trigger terrorism, especially for African Americans like the case of Emmett Till, who was murdered for allegedly flirting with a white woman, Carolyn Bryant.

His killers were acquitted by an all-white jury even when they admitted to the murder. Later in 2017, on her deathbed, Carolyn Bryant admitted that she had lied. This and several other reasons explain why my African American colleagues use the phrase *"When a white woman cries, a black man gets hurt."*

Being ignorant or insensitive to this history is a good example of white centrality, lack of racial humility, and individualism. Why do white women cry during interactions? The reason varies; not being aware that white racism is inevitable, we see feedback as a moral judgment, which often hurts our feelings.

When a white woman cries about some aspects of racism, whether intended or not, all attention is diverted to her immediately, demanding energy, time, as well as attention from all those in the room instead of focusing on how to ameliorate racism. At the same time, the people of color are again abandoned and blamed.

Also, white men are racially fragile. However, I haven't seen their fragility manifest in cross-racial discussions as actual crying. In most cases, their fragility manifests as varying forms of dominance and intimidation which include:

- Arrogant and disingenuous invalidation of racial inequality via "just playing the devil's advocate."
- Controlling the conversation by speaking first, last, and also most often.
- Simplistic and presumptuous proclamations of "the answer" to racism.
- Hostile body language.
- Silence and withdrawal.

- Intellectualizing and distancing.

These moves and several others take race off the table completely and assist white men in retaining control of the discussion. It also helps them to end the challenge to their positions and reassert their dominance. The racist system is one that is reproduced automatically because racism doesn't rely mainly on individual actors. If we must interrupt it, then we need to recognize and challenge the norms, institutions, and structures that are kept in place.

I imagine that some tears are appreciated since they can validate and also bear witness to the pains associated with racism for people of color. But when I cry, I make efforts to be very thoughtful regarding how and the reason why I cry. I try to cry quietly so that I don't end up taking up more space, and when I discover that people are rushing to comfort me, I don't accept it; I just inform them that I'm fine, so we need to move on.

The Men Who Love Us

Also, it's crucial to point out in addition to the general dynamics we've discussed that the tears of white women in cross-racial discussions affect men in very specific ways. I've seen our tears manipulate men of all races through the result of this manipulation are not always the same. When it comes to race and gender hierarchy, white men occupy the highest positions. So, they possess the power to define their reality as well as that of others.

Men of color may come to the aid of white women in these exchanges, and this may be caused by their conditioning under sexism and patriarchy. We must endeavor to examine our responses toward the emotions of other people and the ways they reinscribe race as well as gender hierarchies. We must bear in mind that our racial socialization causes us to repeat racist behavior regardless of our self-image or intentions. **So, we need to continuously ask how our racism manifests, and not if it manifests.**

Chapter 12: WHERE DO WE GO FROM HERE?

Key Takeaways:

- ✓ When our fundamental understanding of racism is transformed, our assumptions will be transformed as well, and this, will, in turn, change the resultant behaviors.
- ✓ To break free from the conditioning of whiteness, whites must discover what they can do and find awesome content written both by white people as well as people of color.
- ✓ When it comes to interrupting my white fragility, welcoming feedback, and understanding that feedback is a good sign in the relationship is crucial.

I earlier identified some of the common emotions, claims, behaviors as well as underlying assumptions of white fragility. The focus of this chapter is to consider how those elements can change if we changed our racial paradigm.

Daily, people of color get various forms of defensive reaction from whites when they are challenged. This also explains why people of color often prefer not to talk to us. Based on the transformed paradigm, we often have different feelings anytime we're given feedback on our unaware racist patterns. It could be feelings of:

- Excitement

- Compassion
- Gratitude
- Guilt
- Motivation
- Discomfort
- Interest

We often engage in various kinds of behaviors when we have the feelings listed above. Some of the behaviors include:

- Apology
- Engaging
- Reflection
- Grappling
- Seeking more understanding
- Listening
- Believing

A look at these claims doesn't characterize us as people that are falsely accused; they suggest openness and humility. So, some of the positive claims we might make any time we have these feelings and engage in the behaviors listed earlier are:

- This is very helpful.
- I appreciate this feedback.
- I will focus on the message rather than the messenger.
- Oops!

- It's my responsibility to resist defensiveness and complacency.
- I need to build my capacity to endure discomfort and also bear witness to the pain of racism.
- This is difficult but crucial and stimulating.

Since these feelings, behaviors, and claims are just too rare, they will be less familiar to readers. However, when our fundamental understanding of racism is transformed, our assumptions will be transformed as well, and this will, in turn, change the resultant behaviors.

Undoubtedly, there would be a significant difference in our interactions, norms, environment as well as policies if our assumptions look like the ones listed below:

- White people have blind spots on racism, and I also have blind spots on racism too.
- Whether I'm good or bad isn't relevant.
- Every one of us has been socialized into the system of racism.
- Racism is complex, and I don't need to understand every nuance of the feedback to validate the feedback.
- Feedback on white racism is not easy to give, so how I'm given the feedback isn't as important as the feedback itself.
- The cure for guilt is action.

- I don't have to confuse comfort with safety. As a white, I'm safe during discussions of racism.
- There is nothing that exempts me from the forces of racism
- People of color are being hurt (and even killed) because of racism. So, interrupting, it is more crucial than my ego, self-image, or feelings.

These assumptions are capable of interrupting racism in several ways, like:

- Allow for growth
- Reduce our defensiveness
- Demonstrate our curiosity and humility
- Help to stretch our worldview
- Demonstrate our vulnerability
- Interrupt privilege-protecting comfort
- Ensure action
- Interrupt internalized superiority
- Show that we practice the things we profess to value.

Anytime whites ask me about what they should do regarding racism and white fragility, I usually ask a question; *"What has enabled you to become a fully educated and professional adult without knowing about the issue of racism?"* This question is simple; how on earth have we managed not to be aware even when the information is right there in front of us? If we take what people of color have been telling us for years seriously and come up with all the ways we have come this far without knowing what to do; then the guide will be right there before us.

Then go ahead and do whatever it takes for you to internalize the assumptions made earlier. It would change our interpersonal relationships as well as our institutions. Also, you can take the initiative and get the answers on your own. To break free from the conditioning of whiteness, whites must discover what they can do, and we can find awesome content written both by white people as well as people of color, search for it.

Going Forward

Earlier in chapter four, I advised that readers shouldn't look up to people of color for racial education. So, how do we get the needed education? There are various interconnected ways we can get it, from films, websites, books, and other sources available. A good number of people of color have been teaching whites about racism for ages, but our lack of motivation has hindered us from receiving it. So, we can demand it in schools, universities, and we can also get involved with multiracial organizations as well as white organizations that are working for racial justice.

I think the most powerful lesson that I've learned so far when it comes to interrupting my white fragility is welcoming feedback and understanding that feedback is a good sign in the relationship.

I understand that I can never be completely free from racism and can never stop learning. But there are certain things that I can do anytime my white fragility appears. I can adopt certain constructive responses like:

- Breathe
- Listen
- Reflect
- Go back to the list of underlying assumptions earlier shared in this chapter
- Find someone that has a stronger analysis when feeling confused
- Spend enough time to process your feelings and don't return to the situation as well as the persons involved.

We can interrupt our white fragility and even develop the capacity to sustain cross-racial honesty. This can be achieved by being willing to tolerate the discomfort that comes with getting an appraisal that's honest and talking about our internalized superiority as well as a racial privilege.

A positive white identity is one of the approaches to anti-racial work. It's suggested that we can develop a positive identity by reclaiming our cultural heritage, which was lost during assimilation into whiteness for European ethnics. However, since white identity is inherently racist – whites don't exist outside the system of white supremacy – a positive white identity is not a possible goal. So, we can strive to be "less white" or racially oppressive, and this requires that we become more racially aware and to get more information about racism.

In Conclusion

Undoubtedly, the current system's default is the reproduction of racial inequality. You can find it in various institutions that were designed to reproduce racial inequality efficiently – the schools in the US are effective in executing this task. All that the system needs to continue reproducing racial inequality is for whites to be nice and smile at people of color and go to lunch together on occasion.

Well, I'm not suggesting that whites shouldn't be nice since it's better than being mean. However, niceness isn't courageous because it can't get racism to the table and leave it on the table when whites want it off. It takes courage and intentionality to interrupt racism, and the interruption isn't complacent. So, to answer the question, *"where do we go from here?"* I would suggest that we should never consider ourselves as those that have finished with our learning.

Even if it was possible to challenge all the racism and superiority that we have internalized easily and quickly, you should understand that our racism would be easily reinforced because we're living in the culture. Always be ready to receive feedback on your patterns and unexamined assumptions because the process is a messy and lifelong one, but crucial to help align our professed values with our true actions.